NAMED

THE DISCIPLES

A WORKBOOK FOR INDIVIDUALS AND SMALL GROUPS

ISBN: 978-0-8341-3052-4

Contributors for *Named: The Disciples* include Katie Savage, Annie Carter, Joseph Bentz, Merritt Nielson, and Julie Joiner.

CONTENTS

INTRODUCTION

Noah, The Woman at the Well, Thomas, Hagar; these men and women are more than just names in Bible stories. They were flesh and blood people. And in seeing how God moved in their lives, we can see him moving in ours. We can hear him call us by name.

Named is a 6-week small group resource that tells the story of people from scripture through a new lens—exploring the mystery of faith with a literary touch. Each series introduces 6 different people from the Bible, unpacking one person's story every week.

This workbook has original stories that are accompanied by historical context for the characters and the times they lived in, insight into how they fit into God's story, and discussion questions to help participants see how God's story works in them. This is a unique opportunity for your group to engage the Scriptures both personally, and as a community. Through the power of history-based stories, you'll see the truth of how God works. Not just in ancient times and in other people, but how he works today and in us all. Become acquainted with the people identified by God in a story as particular as yours.

HOW TO GET THE MOST OUT OF THIS STUDY

In this workbook you will find six narrative stories about some of the men Jesus asked to be his disciples. These flawed men were the ones who Jesus called to ministry with him. Each week you'll read about a different disciple in preparation for your time together with your small group.

The narratives are written to help you to begin to think about how these individuals might have been feeling or what they might have been thinking during their story. Each week before you get together with your group, you might want to read the scriptures that the narrative is based on so that you have a full picture of the story. As you work through the reading and journaling in this book, continue to think about the pieces of the stories that find themselves in your life. What can you learn from these stories and apply in your own life?

WHAT YOU'LL FIND IN EACH CHAPTER

CONTEXT

This section will give readers an understanding of what was going on around the person at the time of the story. Historical, societal, and religious background are given to help readers put themselves in the shoes of those whose stories they are about to read.

STORY

The narratives told in this study attempt to get inside the heads of those whose stories we may have heard hundreds of times before. The writers of these pieces have attempted, through research and reflection, to give us a brief glimpse into what these people might have been thinking and how they might have felt. As you read or listen to the story each week look for places where you can relate to the story—God's story.

PLACE IN GOD'S STORY

This section will give you a short description of how God's story found its place in this individual.

THE STORY FINDS ITS PLACE IN ME

These questions are designed to help you reflect on what you've read in order to find yourself in God's narrative. There is plenty of space available for journaling.

WRITERS

Katie Savage is the author of *Whirlybirds and Ordinary Times: Reflections on Faith and the Changing of Seasons*. She and her husband Scott live in Kansas City with their two children.

Julie Joiner is a writer and counselor living in California. She ministers as an intern counselor for New Vision Counseling Center, writer, mom of two grown daughters, and wife of Jim—a man of ministry.

Annie Carter grew up in Oklahoma with her parents and two older sisters. She is a student at The Writers Studio in New York. She currently lives in New York City with her cat, Olive.

Joseph Bentz is a professor of English at Azusa Pacific University. He lives with his wife and two children in Southern California. His blog, Life of the Mind and Soul, appears at his website, www.josephbentz.com.

Merritt Nielson is the director of curriculum for the Church of the Nazarene. He has served as media producer, pastor, missionary, university professor and administrator, and social-service agency director. He and wife Linda have four children and three grandchildren.

PETER

THE HUMBLED • KEY SCRIPTURE PASSAGE:

Mark 14:27-31, 66-72, John 21

HIS CONTEXT

Before Peter was a disciple of Jesus, he was a fisherman by trade. Working with his brother Andrew, and in partnership with the sons of Zebedee, James and John, Peter's fishing operation was probably pretty lucrative. The house believed to be his family's in Capernaum, for instance, is larger than many of the houses that have been excavated in that area. Fishermen in Peter's time were also more educated than we tend to give them credit for. They were probably fluent in Greek, Hebrew, and Aramaic, and proficient in mathematics.

"When Peter was first called, Jesus said to him, 'Follow Me, and I will make you fishers of men.'"

Fishing figures importantly into Peter's relationship with Jesus. Jesus met Peter where he was at—literally and figuratively. Peter's first encounter with Jesus was on his fishing boat. When Peter was first called, Jesus said to him, "Follow Me, and I will make you fishers of men." A similar account of Jesus asking the disciples to throw their nets on the opposite side of the boat also happened near the beginning of Jesus's relationship with the disciples. It is recorded in Luke.

HIS STORY

The sound of the water lapping against the side of our boat was the only thing we heard. The only thing we had heard for hours, maybe. Usually, on nights like that, Peter's voice filled the silence. He was a good fisherman, but he had never been very adept at keeping quiet so as not to frighten the fish. He joked that he didn't want the kind of fish that were scared off at any sound; the bold ones tasted better.

Tonight was different in many ways. We were here again, in the most familiar of places. Familiarity had been scarce lately; for years, maybe, but for weeks especially. We had to adjust our realities completely more than once, first to accommodate a dead leader, teacher, friend; then to accommodate a live one. A living one. A back-from-the-dead one. My faculties and my imagination had never been more stretched, and while the journey had been an incredible one, the sound of the water on the boat felt good and easy right then.

I didn't know if it felt that way to Peter. My brother had never been as fond of the good and easy the way I was. He was drawn to challenge and energy, high risk and high reward. When we were kids, he led me to jump off the highest rocks into the sea and venture farther from home than we had ever been, and he kept our parents' hearts in their throats. He was constantly in trouble for saying exactly what he thought and doing exactly what he felt like doing. I admired that about him then, and I still did, but his mouth also made me nervous. I've said some embarrassing things, sure. Haven't we all? But I've been embarrassed by Peter's words far worse and far more often.

It caught up to him though. He hadn't been the same since the night Jesus died, and it had to do with something he said. If he'd stopped to think even for a few seconds, I knew he wouldn't have denied knowing Christ. But he didn't think. Three times, he didn't think. He was scared. He was confused. Maybe he was even angry. Now, his words were eating him alive.

"Simon," I called him by the name I always have, not because I didn't consider him the "rock" that his new name meant, but rather because he was my brother and calling him anything but Simon seemed strange.

He looked up from the net he was repairing; trying to keep his hands busy. "Andrew."

"You're so quiet. Aren't you feeling any better?"

He snorted and shook his dark hair. "I don't feel any better," he said. "How could I?"

We both looked out at the sea. It was restless and unsettled this early morning, and neither of us was very surprised that we hadn't caught anything.

I know my brother well and I know he had never loved anyone the way he loved Jesus. Criticism usually bounced off of him like rays of the sun, but not now. Now it had sunk deep into his skin, weighing down on his arms, his legs, the lines on his mouth.

"He knew even before I'd done it," he started. But the cast-net was back, empty again.

Peter smoothed the thin ropes in his sea-rough hands, knowing exactly where to gather, how to lay the weights without allowing them to tangle. Before long, he'd thrown the net out again, the circular web undulating expertly through the air like a sea creature itself before hitting the waves, fully flattened. We waited as the net sank and the weights pulled together. After some minutes, someone jumped overboard to haul the net in. We already expected the nothingness he would retrieve. Cast fishing could be so utterly exhausting, the repetitious pulling in and casting out of the nets. Perhaps it was why Peter had wanted to fish by this method tonight. Not much waiting, not much silence. The circles under his eyes told me he wasn't sleeping much anyway.

The other disciples were not nearly as grim as Peter, but they (and I) had no reason to be. While Peter was grieving his own weakness, the rest of us were celebrating Jesus's return from the dead, imagining what his next move might be, and considering the possibilities. But Peter wasn't free to rejoice. I was sure that Peter was obsessing over why Jesus had not even addressed Peter's denial. He confided in me once, after the first time we'd seen the Lord risen, that he could never get his own wickedness completely from his mind. "I'm as bad as Judas," he'd said. "The Savior is back from the grave, and all I can think about is when he's going to condemn me forever."

"Let's try the other side of the boat," Nathanael called to us when the net came up empty again. He gestured casually at the fisherman on the shore who had suggested the change in tactic. "We'll call it a night after this."

Perhaps it was that we were so tired from the fishing, or so used to the fishermen around the Sea of Tiberius giving advice about the best place to cast our nets. Perhaps we still expected him dead. Whatever the reason, not one of us recognized the Savior in that moment.

And, so, one more cast after a night of a thousand futile casts. A perfect circle cutting through the still dark sky, as usual, but this time on the right side of the boat. After the net had had time to settle on the floor of the sea, Thomas jumped in to collect it. When his head emerged from the water, his grin was sparkling. He threw a wriggling fish at us.

"I'm going to need some help," was all he said. The boat hummed with activity.

"The Savior," I heard John whisper. As he said it, something in Peter's expression changed, and I saw him throw his tunic on over his naked torso.

He dived into the water, away from the bursting net, toward Jesus. The sun was just peeking up over the horizon. —KS

"Criticism usually bounced off of him like rays of the sun, but not now. Now it had sunk deep into his skin, weighing down on his arms, his legs, the lines on his mouth."

HIS PLACE IN GOD'S STORY

Peter is known for his impulsiveness. He asks questions of Jesus that sometimes seem rash and not entirely thought out, and he says things that many of us may think but would never speak aloud. This quality is what many believers seem to appreciate about the disciple. It certainly makes him a key player in many of the Gospel narratives: he rebukes Jesus for trying to wash his feet, then commands him to instead wash his whole body; he begs Jesus to help him walk on water, he blurts out requests for Jesus to explain his parables, he swears he will never deny Jesus and then, in fear, does just that; when Jesus hints at what Peter's future might hold, Peter wants to know if John's will be as harrowing as his or if John will get off easy. And while it's easy to write off Peter's impulsiveness as a character flaw ("foot-in-mouth" disease, as it's sometimes jokingly called), it also shows vulnerability and honesty—the kind of trust that we reserve only for those closest to us. We have room to say stupid things because we know that our statements will be met with grace and understanding rather than harsh judgment and immediate criticism.

". . . while it's easy to write off Peter's impulsiveness as a character flaw ("foot-in-mouth" disease, as it's sometimes jokingly called), it also shows vulnerability and honesty"

The story of the 153 fishes, as this narrative is often called, is followed by one of the most intimate scenes recorded in the Bible between Peter and Jesus. They are sitting together by a fire when Jesus asks Peter, three times, to declare his love for Him. It is as if He's helping Peter make amends for his denial. Three times, Jesus responds by commissioning Peter to "feed my sheep." And, from what we know of Peter's future ministry, he takes Jesus seriously on this command. Peter goes on to become one of the most important figures in the early Christian community. He is a pastor, with his most memorable sermon given at Pentecost, he is a missionary, especially important in the decision to evangelize to the Gentiles, and he is an activist, picking up where Jesus leaves off challenging the religious authorities of the day. He is said to have been martyred on a cross, upside-down because he felt himself unworthy to die the same way that Jesus did.

THE STORY FINDS ITS PLACE IN ME

1. What parts of Peter's story find their place in you?

2. How do you think Peter's betrayal of Jesus differs from Judas'?

3. Were you ever in a position where you felt you needed a second chance with God? Write about it.

4. Why do you think Peter's first response when he recognizes Jesus is to swim toward him?

5. In Matthew, Jesus says, “You are Peter, and upon this rock I will build My church.” How do you think Peter’s experience with denying Jesus and being forgiven helped to prepare him for this charge?

NOTES

JOHN

THE STEADFAST • KEY SCRIPTURE PASSAGE:

Revelation 1:1-10; John 21:20-23

HIS CONTEXT

By the end of John's ministry, he is recorded as the last living disciple of the twelve who lived with Jesus. John was one of the youngest of the twelve, and his ministry had been a rich and fruitful one. However, in his old age he was exiled to the island of Patmos, removed from both his home and the cities where he had been ministering.

> "We know now, of course, that those letters are canonized as New Testament gospel and epistles."

During this period of time, John spent much of his days doing what we may consider mundane, writing letters and praying. We know now, of course, that those letters are canonized as New Testament gospel and epistles. Most scholars believe that he died peacefully in Ephesus after recording the revelation.

HIS STORY

He sat in the dust with his back against the stone and his legs stretched out in front of him with the sun warming his bare feet. He had collected a small handful of figs and was taking a bit out of each one and lining them up from where he sat over to his right where the cat was crouched. The soft pink insides of the figs stood out like gems in the sandy earth and the sweetness drew small flies and honey bees. But the cat did not come. The juice of the fruit made his fingers sticky and he wiped them across his linen shirting and then called softly to the small cat.

"Don't be afraid."

He took the fig closest to him and tossed it toward the brambles. The cat's ears flattened down low over its cheeks. From the side of the hill where he sat the man looked out and watched the clouds break apart over the sea. It was some irrelevant hour of the afternoon and the sun was changing colors. A breeze blew. Shadows stretched out and yawned. Another day had come and gone and he gave thanks. He turned back to the cat.

"We should be friends," he said. "I could tell you such stories."

There was an oldness about the man more than physical. Something hung on him like bonfire smoke. He rested his head on the curve of the stone where it opened up to the mouth of the cave and he looked out to the horizon. The milky colors of the landscape around him. The hills below him and the sea beyond, it all looking like the silt-covered bottom of the sea. His mind wandered.

He thought of names and places. Hillsides alight with the glory of heaven. The dark bedroom where a little girl woke from death. He could see their faces and it made him miss their company. He knew a man would see much if he lived forever. The coastline itself might shift under the weight of the sea. He wondered what else would change. The fishing ships. The language he spoke. The wild cat itself might cease to exist. What would happen to his own body if it would not die?

He sat still this way thinking for so long that the sun sank to evening and the cat made a move and came out from the rockrose bushes and the delicate blossoms pulled away from their stems and when the tawny animal was out in the open the blooms stuck to its fur and covered it like a child's feast day gift. The man watched the cat move around the figs and lean in close to smell them keeping its eyes on the man all the while. Once the cat hunched to taste the fruit John joined him and reached out to take the nearest fig but the cat was spooked and shot out into the shadows and was gone. John turned the fig over his hand a few times before saying a blessing over it and then eating it alone.

The feeling of isolation came and went in ebbs and flows. In the mornings he woke up with the sun. In the afternoons he wrote and prayed. And by evening he lay in the dark of the cave sometimes weeping and not always sure why. He could not seem to shake the dizzy feeling of having been cut loose from a mooring. Like a little boat that floats tethered to a larger ship and one day gets cut away at the ropes. He feared drifting out to sea.

From where he sat he found a small white stone in the dirt beside him. He picked it up and ran his thumb over the surface. It was smooth and flat in his palm and he thought it would have made a good skipping stone. He flipped the stone over in his hand to the clean, pale side that had been in the sun and then he started writing in the dirt the names of each of the men he had ministered with some 50 or so years ago. He got up on his knees and reached over to his right to scrawl one name and then out in front to write another. The words made a sort of semicircle around him and he found he was writing their names in the order they used to sit at a dinner table. It made him smile to think how families seem to always take the same seats at the table.

He tilted back on his heels and wrote a final name to his left next to where he sat. He stared at it a while before sitting back to the ground against the wall and stretching his legs out in front, scraping a line through the dirt and inadvertently blotting out the name across from him. He rested his hands in his lap and looked up at the gathering clouds. He thought of them looking down watching him hold court with a collection of imaginary friends and this made him laugh.

He clapped his hands together and the dust scattered and shimmered in the gold light. He brushed the dust off of his tunic and stood up from the ground. He walked out to where the hill started to drop away and looked down on the narrow streets by the sea. He counted the days on his fingers and remembered it was the Lord's Day. He turned his good ear to the town below and could hear singing from somewhere in the tangle of Cyprus trees. He turned and went into the shallow cave where he kept a few belongings including a large woolen blanket that he took up and wrapped over his shoulders against the evening breeze and then he took a well-used tallow candle from the floor and carried it out into the open with a flint stone.

The names of his friends were still written in the dust and he stepped around them carefully. He bent next to the rockrose bush and struck the stone until it sparked and lit the candle and he stood in the shadow of coming night and prayed aloud.

"Avinu shebashamayim, yitkadesh shimkha (Our Father which art in heaven, hallowed be thy name.)"

He lifted his hands up into the air and opened his palms to the heavens and started to sing. The sound of the waves hummed in time to his song and he heard the voices below seem to rise up to meet him. If this alone were how he would spend eternity, he knew it would not be in vain. In that same moment he heard a noise behind him like a tree splitting in two and the shadows evaporated into a bright sheen of light and John dropped to his knees and turned to see what had come to shake his island of exile. —AC

"He thought of names and places. Hillsides alight with the glory of heaven. The dark bedroom where a little girl woke from death. He could see their faces and it made him miss their company."

HIS PLACE IN GOD'S STORY

It is innate in the human experience that we are subjected to waiting. Everything from waiting in line at the Post Office to waiting out an often long and arduous stretch of unemployment. And in the Christian walk, waiting through times of unanswered prayer or confusion can begin to take a toll on our lives. The thing to remember about John's story is that he too experienced that keen sense of, "What now?" As the last living disciple, all the men, and presumably women, he had been working with over the years had gone on before him.

Additionally, there was some speculation of John's immortality at that time. In John 21:22 when Peter asked Jesus about John's future, Jesus responded by telling Peter that if He wanted John to remain alive until the return of Christ, he would. Now compound a statement like that with the fact that John was in fact the last living disciple and that historians record that, prior to being exiled to Patmos, John had been taken to Rome and thrown into a vat of boiling oil and had survived unscathed. At that point, it would be understandable to presume that John himself may have begun to wonder if he would in fact live forever. And what a daunting thought, already so late in life. And so John's waiting begins.

In our times of waiting, we can be tempted to throw the towel in. However, we recall that Jesus Himself spent the first 30 years of His life in anticipation of the last three. And in the same way, toward what would prove to be the end of John's life, he is chosen to witness one of the most tremendous experiences recorded in the Bible, the vision that would become the book of Revelation.

THE STORY FINDS ITS PLACE IN ME

1. What parts of John's story find their place in you?

2. Consider the areas of your life where you are still experiencing waiting or unanswered requests. Take a moment to thank God that you are not forgotten and that you have been promised a plan.

3. Reframe what you feel you are waiting for into the context of hope. Praise God for what is ahead and, in prayer today, speak to Him about sustaining you in times of uncertainty as well as thanking Him for the evidence of His work all around you, in big and small ways.

4. John might have questioned God's direction for his life and given in to negative thoughts of how things might have been. Instead he focused on God. How might this choice effect the situations you are waiting on God in?

5. In exile on the island of Patmos John must have had some lonely moments while waiting on God's next move in his life. What can we do when the waiting seems lonely and long?

NOTES

ANDREW

THE HUNGRY • KEY SCRIPTURE PASSAGES:

John 6:1-14

HIS CONTEXT

The feeding of the 5,000, in which Andrew plays a significant role, is the only miracle of Jesus to be recorded in all four gospels. Although Andrew is not one of the more well-known disciples, he is mentioned several times in Scripture, and his actions make a difference. In most of the scenes in which he is named, he is shown bringing someone to Jesus. (John 1:41-42, 6:8-14, and 12:20-22)

In all these cases, the significance of Andrew's actions is not that he made an argument in favor of Jesus or that he tried to push any agenda of his own. It was enough that he simply ushered these people into Jesus' presence, and Jesus did the rest.

> "The conversation they had with Jesus on that day is not recorded, but by the end of it, Andrew was convinced, 'We have found the Messiah.'"

Before following Jesus, Andrew was a disciple of John the Baptist. When John looked at Jesus and declared that He was the Lamb of God, Andrew and another disciple followed Jesus as he walked away. Jesus turned around and asked, "What do you want?" How would any of us answer such a question coming from Jesus? Were they surprised by this sudden direct attention from him? Their response was simple and respectful. They called him "Rabbi," or Teacher, and asked, "Where are you staying?" Jesus answered, "Come and you will see." They went and spent the day with him. The conversation they had with Jesus on that day is not recorded, but by the end of it, Andrew was convinced, "We have found the Messiah." (John 1:35-41).

HIS STORY

I buried John the Baptist. He died a horrible death—beheading—and I could hardly bear the thought of it. Without John, I never would have met the Messiah. And now here was his mutilated body, discarded in the dirt.

Some of the other disciples and I buried John, and then we went and told Jesus. He was as devastated as we were. All of us were grieving yet we had no space to grieve. Every day, wherever we went, the crowds pressed in, eager for healing, and hungry (or at least curious) about the message of the gospel. Whenever I was near Jesus, I felt more like a bodyguard than a disciple. The people pushed toward him almost desperately at times. They just wanted to get close—to hear him, to touch him, or even to catch a glimpse of him through the throng. Some of the disciples, like my brother Simon Peter, thrived in the crowds, but I had a harder time with them. Sometimes I got so tired of being jostled and pushed by the smelly, shouting bodies that I wanted to run as far as I could and find any spot where I could be alone and unbothered for at least an hour.

Jesus knew we needed to get away to grieve and pray. He decided to take us to a remote spot across the Sea of Galilee. But people saw us getting into the boats—some even tried to get on board with us—and word spread of what we were doing. Lots of them decided to follow us by running and walking north along the shore and then down to where we would land. They picked up even more people along the way. As we got closer to shore, the people shouted and waved.

I was getting grouchy and hungry, and I prayed someone would talk Jesus into somehow getting rid of all these people. Only he could do it, even though I didn't know how. As I was helping to secure the boat, I looked up to see Jesus wading into the throng, not reluctantly, but as if he had invited everyone there. He touched as many as he could, putting his hands on their heads the way he does. He even picked up one little boy from the dirt after the crowd practically trampled him. These people loved him. We were stuck with them now, and I wasn't happy about it.

I don't mean to sound harsh. I love people too. I'm one of Jesus' disciples, after all. I know what he teaches about love. But there are limits to what we can endure. What good are we to others if we're so tired and hungry we can barely think straight? And was it really loving for us to keep the crowd out here in the middle of nowhere, with no food or drink? They hadn't prepared for this, and neither had we.

I pulled Peter aside and said, "We have to do something about these crowds. It'll be dark before long, and we'll have several thousand hungry people on our hands! What happens then?"

Peter shrugged. "Tell Jesus."

I loved Jesus, and revered him, but I was still a little shy around him sometimes, especially when it came to giving him advice. Who was I to say we should disperse the crowd? Surely Jesus could see just as well as I that hordes of people were streaming in from every direction now. Where were they all coming from?

Jesus spoke from the top of the hill, and everyone was mesmerized. He seemed oblivious to the lateness of the day and all the practical problems. But he would stop before long, and then everyone would realize they were hungry, and we would face a riot.

I decided to push through and talk to Jesus. My own hunger and weariness were making me bolder than usual. I pushed past people toward the top of the hill where Jesus taught.

Before I could reach him, someone grabbed my arm and pulled me hard to the side. He was just a kid, a teenager.

"I'm so sorry, sir," he said. "I just wanted to stop you; to talk to you. Please. I want to meet him. I'll do anything. I'll give anything." He held out the only possession he carried, a beat-up little basket. "Here," he said. "It's all I have."

"What is it?"

"Food. I'll give it to him. I'll give it to you if you'll just introduce me."

"How much is in there?"

"Two fish and five loaves of bread."

I smiled. The boy didn't have much, but the intensity of his desire to see Jesus reminded me of my own first encounter with him, when I just had to follow him and talk to him, even though he hadn't invited me to. When Jesus had turned to me that day and asked, "What do you seek?," all I could think to say was "Rabbi, where are you staying?" That wasn't what I really wanted to ask at all. Jesus knew that, I think. He smiled and said, "Come and see," and by the end of that day spent with him, I knew I had found the Messiah.

By the time we reached the top of the hill, Jesus had stopped his teaching, and to my surprise he walked right up to me, as if he were expecting me. Philip was there too, and before I could say anything, Jesus asked, "How are we to buy bread so we can feed all these people?"

Philip threw up his hands in a helpless gesture. "Two hundred denarii would not buy enough bread to feed even a fraction of them." Not that we had anywhere near that kind of money, nor anywhere to buy the bread from even if we did.

Before I even had time to think about what I was saying, I blurted out, "I have a boy here with two fish and five barley loaves."

Then Jesus gave me that look. He has done it before. I had no idea what he was thinking, but he looked right through me, as if the two of us were alone on that hill, and this was some important moment, but I had no idea why.

I added, rather lamely, "But how far will so little food go among so many people?" I didn't want him to think I expected that to feed everybody. But we had to do something.

Jesus reached out and took the scraggly basket from the boy, who was eagerly holding it out to him. You would have thought the kid was handing over a huge feast, the way both of them acted. Jesus looked at me and the rest of the disciples nearby and, as if all our problems had been resolved, said, "Ask everybody to sit down."

Jesus took the boy's food and held it up and gave thanks for it. He started passing it around. Given the small amount, I would have at least chopped it into tiny pieces, but Jesus gave it freely and let people take whatever they wanted.

He turned back to those who wanted to talk to him, and the food spread throughout the crowd. It took us awhile to realize what was happening, but no one went hungry that day. The food spread and spread, and everyone had their fill. As if to make sure we didn't miss the significance of what was happening, Jesus told us to gather up all the food that was left, and we filled twelve baskets!

Jesus could have simply commanded all that food into existence on his own if he had chosen to. But instead, he took what that kid brought him and made something more of it. I brought him a boy with a little bread and fish, and he fed thousands. —JB

"I smiled. The boy didn't have much, but the intensity of his desire to see Jesus reminded me of my own first encounter with him."

HIS PLACE IN GOD'S STORY

When Andrew brought to Jesus the boy with the fish and the small amount of bread, he showed faith in Jesus' ability to multiply that offering to accomplish his purposes. The feeding of the 5,000 bears similarities to other stories in the Bible in which God took a small amount of food that people offered and made it adequate to fulfill the need at hand. Another prominent example is in 2 Kings 4. When a man comes to Elisha with twenty loaves of bread, Elisha tells him to give it to the people to eat. "How can I set this before a hundred men?" the man asks. Elisha's answer sounds very much like Jesus' answer in the feeding of the 5,000. Elisha says, "Give it to the people to eat. For this is what the Lord says: 'They will eat and have some left over.'" When the man obeys, that is exactly what happens (2 Kings 4:42-44).

Earlier in 2 Kings, Elisha is part of another story in which God multiplies a small amount that someone possesses. A widow comes to him pleading for help in staving off a creditor who wants to take her boys as slaves. Elisha asks her what she has, and she tells him she has nothing except a little oil, but God stretches what little she has to exceed her needs. (2 Kings 4:1-7).

In all these stories, God does not start from scratch in producing the miracle. Instead, he starts with the small amount that people make available to him, and He multiplies it. If they had not given that small amount, the miracle would not have happened. Andrew understands this principle and does not hesitate to bring the boy's meager lunch to Jesus, even though the crowd is huge.

THE STORY FINDS ITS PLACE IN ME

1. What parts of Andrew's story find their place in you?

2. Put yourself in Andrew's place. Would you have brought the boy to Jesus? Would his offering have seemed too small to bother with? What do you think led Andrew to take the boy and his food to Jesus? In your own life, are you ever tempted to withhold what you have to offer in service to Christ because it seems too insignificant?

3. Can you remember examples in which God took something small and multiplied it for His purposes? Do those stories include someone like Andrew, who trusted God for the outcome even though in purely human terms the problem seemed insurmountable?

4. In most of the stories in the Bible that feature Andrew, he is shown bringing people to Jesus. He doesn't use argument or persuasion or explanation about Jesus—he simply leads them into Jesus' presence. Are there ways in which you as a Christian can lead people into Jesus' presence, no matter how shy or inarticulate you may think you are?

5. Andrew saw this miracle of God's abundance. God not only solved the immediate problem, but He provided even more than they needed. What examples of God's abundance have you enjoyed, when He not only fulfills your request but goes beyond what you would have dared to ask?

NOTES

THOMAS

THE MARTYR • KEY SCRIPTURES:

Matthew 10:3; Mark 3:18; Luke 6:12-16; John 11:7-16; 14:1-6; 20:24-29; 21:1-12; Acts 1:12-14

HIS CONTEXT

This account of the apostolic mission and martyrdom of Thomas is suggested by the biblical accounts of his life with Jesus and by long-standing church tradition. In a broad sense it fits the definition of historical fiction, with biblical allusions within the story drawn directly from the gospel narratives. As a result of persecution in Jerusalem (Acts 8:1-3; 9:1-2; 12:1-4), the book of Acts suggests that early Christians scattered (Acts 8:4; 8:26). Tradition holds that with the blessing of Peter, Thomas headed east from Jerusalem traveling through what is now Jordan, Saudi Arabia, Iraq, Iran, and finally reaching India. If Paul did indeed take his apostolic mission as far as Spain (Romans 15:24), Thomas traveled as far to the east as Paul did to the west, missionary journeys encompassing nearly 2,500 miles in each direction.

A church community in Malabar on the southwest coast of India claims a direct spiritual lineage from those Christians who were converted by the ministry of Thomas. Tracing its origins to AD 52, the Mar Thoma Syrian Church of Malabar is one of the oldest denominations of Christianity. The Church defines itself as apostolic in origin, universal in nature, biblical in faith, evangelical in principle, ecumenical in outlook, oriental in worship, democratic in function, and episcopal in character. Headquartered at Thiruvalla in Kerala, India, the church has followers across the globe.

Church tradition holds that Thomas was martyred in AD 72 by his Hindu opposition. According to this same tradition, he was executed with a lance and buried near Madras.

HIS STORY

A bead of sweat trickled down the weathered face of the prisoner and disappeared into his beard. White-haired, but still ruggedly built, the bound seventy-year-old captive, accompanied by two guards, walked erect into a small courtyard behind a group of pagan temples in Malabar. He scanned the distant sky. A sliver of moon and a single star hung in the darkness above the slice of pink that rimmed the horizon announcing the dawn of another day in the humid southwestern coast of the Indian peninsula.

One of his guards stripped off his tunic. The other guard pushed him against a tall wooden picket, while the first yanked his arms and wrapped them around the stake. Together, they bound him with metal-studded leather thongs that cut deeply into his wrists and forearms. The soldiers passed a thick rope over his chest and upper arms, pulling it so tightly that his shoulders curved backward and his torso jutted out like the prow of a boat. Sharp pain made him wince, but he said nothing.

His thoughts raced back forty years to an early morning when the Nazarene Rabbi had come to his group of followers after a night of prayer. The prisoner remembered the surprise that welled up in his chest at being chosen from among such a large band to form the small circle of twelve.

"Thomas," the Rabbi said, "I want you with us."

The invitation had been warm, strong, spiritually invigorating. The affairs of his business as both a fisherman and a master craftsman in Capernaum of Galilee were suddenly much less important. What he was hearing from the Rabbi ignited a burst of spiritual fervor as if he were being birthed into a new life.

Those had been happy days, walking and talking and eating together with Jesus and the other eleven. "Astounding days, good days," he thought. There had been threats on the Master's life, but He had slipped away across the Jordan to

"If there had ever been a time when he had been strong and bold like the Master, it was that moment. Courage to die, that's what he needed right now."

elude those who were intent on arresting Him. Then the courier had come with news of Lazarus's death, and Jesus was ready to walk right back into certain danger. Everyone had tried to dissuade Him, but He was determined to be with Mary and Martha in their grieving. "Let's go too—and die with Jesus," Thomas had challenged James and John. If there had ever been a time when he had been strong and bold like the Master, it was that moment. Courage to die, that's what he needed right now.

Thomas opened his eyes. Across the courtyard, three burly soldiers had assembled, each with a javelin sporting a black cord tied at its neck. They joked among themselves, making coarse, obscene gestures as they stared at him. He looked away, his eyes focusing on an iron fence that separated the courtyard from a narrow cobblestone alley. He watched a group of people assembling there, when suddenly one raised a small makeshift cross high over his head. Now he recognized them. They were his people, pious Jews and enlightened Hindus who had become convinced of the gospel about Jesus of Nazareth because of his witness, and had joined his Nazraani Margam, Nazarenes of the Way. The believers from his fledgling congregation stood silently, prayerfully. He was heartened by their presence.

The tallest soldier raised his lance, cocked his arm, and in one swift forward movement, he propelled it forward. The razor sharp javelin whistled toward Thomas and tore through the firm pectoral muscle below his right collar bone, next to the socket of his shoulder. The tip exited through his back.

"Jesus, be merciful to me," he whispered.

He was transported to a room with the other apostles some forty years earlier. "I am going away and you know where I am going," Jesus was saying. It was the night before His crucifixion. Thomas heard himself blurting out, "No, we don't, Lord. We haven't any idea where you are going, so how can we know the way?"

Jesus had locked eyes with him. "I AM the Way, the Truth, and the Life."

He didn't see the second lance coming. It tore through his inner left thigh and pinned it to the wooden stake to which he was bound. The faces of hundreds of Christians in the Asian subcontinent who had become followers of the Way since his arrival in Muziris twenty years earlier passed before his eyes. No regrets.

"My Lord . . ."

The sun was slowly ascending. He was back in a room behind locked doors with his brother disciples. He felt again the dark doubt that had plagued him after some had claimed that the Rabbi had risen from the dead. He had wanted proof—visible nail prints and an open scar where the Roman lance had pierced the heart of Jesus.

"Put your finger here, Thomas. Slip your hand into the wound in my side. Don't be faithless any longer. Believe, Thomas, believe!"

It was as if that moment were happening again. He heard himself whisper aloud what he had blurted out then in that experience of revelation and worship, a personal credo that was forever the signature of his life: "My Lord and my God."

His head fell forward, but he raised it just as the third executioner lifted his javelin, reared back and released it toward its intended mark. It approached him in slow motion, making a searing sound. He was in a boat, fishing with Simon Peter, Nathanael, James and John, and two other disciples. Who was that on the shore calling out to them?

"Friends, have you caught any fish?"

Thomas cupped his hands, "No." The word echoed on the water.

"Throw out your net on the right-hand side of the boat, and you'll get plenty of fish."

It was John who knew first. "It is the Lord!" Then Simon had jumped out of the boat and splashed toward the beach. Thomas had stayed with the others to pull the net filled with fish into shore.

"Lord, forgive them." The javelin struck the rib cage, opening a gaping hole in his flesh and tearing into his heart. His body lurched and slumped to the right as his lifeblood spurted from the wound in his side.

It was finished. There was no memory of the pain. Thomas the Twin was running toward the shore where his Friend stood, waiting for him with arms outstretched and wounds still visible. —MN

HIS PLACE IN GOD'S STORY

Thomas often gets a bad rap as the "doubter" of Christ's bodily resurrection. This piece of historical fiction based on each of the gospel references to Thomas paints another picture.

- Even though Jesus is in danger, He's intent on going to the home of Mary and Martha where their brother Lazarus has died. While the disciples warn Him not to go, it is Thomas who speaks up boldly, "Let us go with him and die with him" (John 11:16).
- In the Upper Room on the night of His crucifixion, Jesus tells His disciples that He is "going away." Then He says, "You know the way to get where I'm going." And it's Thomas who sets up the moment for one of Christ's most evocative statements: "Lord, we don't know where you are going," said Thomas. "How can we know the way?" To which Jesus replies, "I AM the Way, the Truth, and the Life" (John 14:5-6).
- In the Upper Room after the Resurrection, Thomas is not present when Jesus appears to His disciples. When Thomas hears about it, he asks for "proof"—visible wounds in Christ's hands and side. The following week, in that same room, Jesus appears again and shows Thomas His wounds. Thomas utters the first creed of the Church, "My Lord and my God" (John 20:24-29).
- Thomas was among the disciples who decided to go fishing on one particular day following his encounter with Jesus in the Upper Room. He was in the boat with Peter and several other disciples when they heard a voice calling from the shore (John 21:4-5). On that wonderful day, Thomas, along with the other disciples, pulled a net full of fish up onto the beach—153 to be exact.
- Tradition tells us that Thomas traveled all the way to India, evangelizing as he went.

THE STORY FINDS ITS PLACE IN ME

1. What parts of Thomas's story find their place in you?

2. In John 20:28-29, how does Jesus draw the twenty-first-century reader into Thomas's faith with the words, "Have you believed because you have seen me? Blessed are those who have not seen and yet believe."

3. Comment on this observation by St. Gregory the Great: "Thomas's lack of faith did more for our faith than did the faith of the disciples who believed."

4. How does the Thomas narrative of John 11:7-16 show up in the short story, "Martyr of Malabar"? Discuss other ways the stories of Thomas in the gospel of John play themselves out in "Martyr of Malabar."

5. What might it mean to become a spiritual twin of Jesus?

NOTES

MATTHEW

THE CALLED • KEY SCRIPTURE PASSAGES:

Matthew 9:9-13

HIS CONTEXT

During any time period and in any culture, those collecting taxes are criticized and suspect of personal gain with little genuine interest in the needs of a community. When Rome held power in the Middle East, tax collectors did not apply for jobs with a resume full of impressive accomplishments; a contract was awarded the highest bidder. These men, considered thieves and traitors to their own people, would submit a dollar amount to be collected and given to the Roman government. Anything collected above the amount promised the Romans would be pocketed for personal gain. Therefore a tax collector set his own wages. Extremely elevated taxes, not including excessive charges to line the tax collector's pocket, often drove farmers from the land and left villages desolate.

> "It was not that Jesus disagreed, but He chose to befriend tax collectors, prostitutes and other sinners; and all are sinners."

It was not only the tax collector who betrayed his own countrymen; the Jewish aristocrats worked behind the scenes arranging tax collections. Tax collectors were commonly classified with prostitutes and other sinners by the Jewish people, including the Pharisees. It was not that Jesus disagreed, but He chose to befriend tax collectors, prostitutes and other sinners; and all are sinners. To the Pharisee a sinner was an ordinary person who did not adhere to the Pharisaic food laws; they were highly offended at seeing Jesus eat with the sinners.

It was not uncommon for teachers of ancient times to equate health metaphorically with spiritual wholeness and equate disease with opposition and immorality. Jesus knew himself to be the physician of the soul and his response to their Pharisaical challenge was clearly understood. For the orthodox Jew, applying oneself to follow the law implicitly separated them from sinners in their own thinking. But Jesus makes it clear his message is for those who are imperfect, sick, and not for those who are well; the pride of the self-sufficient gives the illusion of health.

HIS STORY

Their words drove sharp into my soul; I hated hearing myself spoken of with such disdain. There I sat with Jesus as my guest, sharing a meal with friends. I cringed at the insolence. Their rude question may have been directed at the Messiah, but the contempt fell hard on those of us who had been soiled by our odious choices. Today my eyes were opened to the filth that cloaked me.

Just hours before the Pharisees tossed their piercing challenge into our feast, I sat inside a tax collector's booth doing what I did everyday: extracting as much money as possible from my neighbors. My parents had named me Levi, but I had not followed a priestly path; no rabbi had chosen me as a talmidim, or disciple. Wrestling to find my way among a culture of fishermen and farmers, I was uncertain of how I fit in.

So I chose money. I gave a bid to the Roman government that I might make a living collecting taxes; I was chosen. I became a puppet for Roman oppression against my own people. Being a tax collector was not considered a respectable job among my Jewish neighbors, but someone had to do the job; from their affliction I grew wealthy without a care.

Now their desperate pleas haunt me. "The crop was not good this year, I do not have enough to feed my family and pay my taxes. I beg of you, sir, please can't you take less?"

Duty to Rome and loyalty to my own purse left me with no compassion. "It is not my problem you did not do your job well. This is the tax you owe, pay it or you will find yourself in prison."

And it was on such a day, right in the middle of my greedy work, Jesus of Nazareth walked by and called me out of my booth and out of my self-constructed life; he invited me to follow him. I can still hear the authority in his voice as he spoke the invitation, "Follow me."

I did.

A crowd of people moved along with him wherever he went like the dust drifting about his feet. All those people competing to be near him and he wanted me to join him, to be his disciple, his talmidim. He chose me.

There was something in his voice, in his presence that compelled me to get up and leave behind everything to follow him. He called me out of a greedy, oppressive career and self-absorbed life. He called me to leave my soiled life and to emulate a life of virtue only he could model. He clipped the strings tied to the service of sin. He freed me to live a life of purpose and compassion. There was no way I would ever understand why, but he chose me. Often since that day my heart has been filled with surprised gratitude at his choosing and accepting me.

He called; I rose, left, and followed. He made the way for me to follow him; putting my foot down on top of his footprint impressed upon the dirt, I wondered how far the implications of my decision would reach. I was used to calculating the cost, but I had no way of knowing the tally of following Jesus. I was used to being an outsider, but when Jesus called out to me to follow him I knew I belonged for the first time. Yet, still I found myself the prey of loathing as a venomous question bit open the flesh of tenderness I had closed off inside of me that I might extract a living from my people and ignore their suffering. I had planned a celebration; they designed a trap for Jesus sending barbs into many of my guests.

Earlier in the day my excitement at being chosen as I am by Jesus, the Messiah, planted a desire in my heart to know him better and to introduce my friends to him. My friends would be curious about the One who could so easily lure me to relinquish the lucrative lifestyle I had so carefully constructed. These thoughts unfolded a plan for a festive meal with Jesus as my guest.

I gave an invitation to Jesus, "Lord, I would be pleased if you would join me and my friends for supper in my home. I want my friends to meet you."

He accepted. Those closest to him would join us as well. Little did I know the Pharisees followed in his shadow for opportunities to find him in contempt of the law. Word was sent out to those I called friends, others detested by the more religious establishment, summoning them to come meet my special guest. A feast was prepared with care and attention to all the details. My servants bustled throughout my dwelling making everything ready for this celebratory event. Jesus had chosen me to be his disciple and my friends were about to have an opportunity to encounter the promised Messiah.

They came. In my excitement a hasty kiss brushed each cheek welcoming guests as they arrived then words of greeting tumbled over into awe as I introduced them to Jesus. I'm not sure any of us truly understood what the excitement was all about. How could we have known what it meant to be a follower of Jesus? Yet he aroused something in our hearts, calling us to something so much better and more than we could imagine.

We reclined at the table; he gave thanks and we ate. We ate and we listened as he spoke. It was in the midst of these unguarded moments, enraptured by his presence, the Pharisees brought their cynicism into the room. They weren't even brave enough to direct their question to Jesus, but instead questioned his disciples about the choice he made. They wanted to know why he was eating with us: tax collectors and sinners.

His compassionate, listening ears did not miss it. He knew their hearts and he knew what their words implied. You should have heard Jesus' response; it was just as sharp, but did not come from a place of pride as much as from a place of truth I was not accustomed to. He said plainly, "I did not come here to take care of healthy people; a physician takes care of the sick."

Oh, but he did not stop there. He told them, "Go figure out what this means: I long for mercy, not the sacrifices of men." I am certain he was sending them back to their studies. He questioned their understanding of the words written by the prophets; words they had used to create a religion impossible to satisfy, even for themselves.

I may still be considered an outsider by the Pharisees and those like them, but this one thing I put my hope in: Jesus is the Messiah prophesied in the Old Testament. He called me. I am a disciple and follower of Jesus. —JJ

"There was no way I would ever understand why, but he chose me. Often since that day my heart has been filled with surprised gratitude at his choosing and accepting me."

HIS PLACE IN GOD'S STORY

In Matthew 9:9 we find Matthew doing what he did everyday: sitting in his tax collector's booth collecting taxes for the Roman government and more to increase his personal wealth. Matthew, a tax collector, hated for the career in which he valued the coin over the people. As a tax collector, not only was he hated for oppressing the people, but he was considered unclean; his work brought him in constant contact with the Gentiles, not to mention his association with the Romans who tyrannized the poor. He was a man whose friends, also sinners, were as hated as he; the orthodox Jews were dead against rubbing elbows with a man who had sold out to the Roman government and robbed their people of a living.

Matthew, whose name means "the gift of God," was born in Galilee where Jesus spent most of his ministry. Matthew's birth name was Levi, after the priestly tribe of Israel, the Levites. But later he was given the name Matthew possibly to memorialize his acceptance of Jesus' call to be his disciple and follow him.

As a witness of Jesus' death, resurrection, and ascension, Matthew's Gospel is focused on showing Jesus to be the Messiah promised in the Old Testament. The fact Matthew was a tax collector is a good indicator he had been educated in Aramaic and Greek.

Matthew presented, for the first time, a group of people who were formed into a culture of faith called the church. He is the only gospel writer to call these followers of Jesus the Church. In his writings, Matthew made it clear that the church is to be inclusive no matter a person's race or social status. It stands to reason Matthew had a heart for all; his former position as a tax collector placed him outside of the acceptable, and except for the grace of Jesus he would not belong to the Church.

THE STORY FINDS ITS PLACE IN ME

1. What parts of Matthew's story find their place in you?

2. How have your past sins contributed to your feeling as if you do not fit into the faith community? Does this feeling come out of your own condemnation and shame, or is it a result of demeaning words and attitudes directed to you from others saved by grace?

3. Matthew was chosen by Jesus and he followed without question. But Matthew also knew what it was like not to be chosen. Write about a time when you were chosen for something special or experienced the feeling of having been chosen by someone.

4. Think back to those first days after you became a follower of Christ. Did others see a difference in you? Did you find yourself wanting to share with all your friends the One who had changed your life and given you peace?

5. Do you ever take time to stop and think how awesome it is that the Creator of the Universe, God, invites you into a personal relationship with him. Close your eyes and think about what this means to you right now and how it has changed the course of your life. (Sit quietly for a few minutes.) What emotions rise up within you as you meditate on his incredible love and grace?

NOTES

BARTHOLOMEW

THE READY • KEY SCRIPTURE PASSAGES:

John 1:43-51

HIS CONTEXT

Bartholomew is referenced by name as a member of one of the twelve disciples in Matthew, Mark and Luke, as well as in Acts after Jesus' ascension. However, it is generally believed by scholars that Bartholomew and Nathanael are the same man. In the gospel of John, Philip's friend the apostle is exclusively referenced as Nathanael. Therefore in John 1:43-51 the disciple referenced as Nathanael is commonly thought to be the same man who is called Bartholomew in the other gospels.

> "However, it is generally believed by scholars that Bartholomew and Nathanael are the same man."

Bartholomew was a fisherman, as were many of the twelve. In Bartholomew's case, he was brought to Christ by his friend Philip. Philip, filled with excitement over what he had witnessed of Jesus, finds his friend and implores him to come and meet the one Moses had written about. And so begins the gathering of the twelve, a catalyst for the fulfillment of Christ's story.

HIS STORY

The walk out of town and up the hill had been hot, and Bartholomew was sweating and dust was starting to stick to his bare calves. His morning had been so unpleasant and he was now so uncomfortable that by the time he reached the fig tree he threw the basket of fish to the ground, tore a handful of leaves from a low branch and then sat down heavily and let out a sigh. The heat was breeding a familiar rage in the dusty streets below, and Bartholomew was not a man eager to welcome confrontation.

As he pulled his boat onto the shore that morning, locals had pushed up around him and pulled at the nets full of fish in the floor of the boat. He told them to wait and he would bring them up the bank, but they wiped grime from their faces with the backs of their hands and called out what they wanted, waving coins in the air. He told them to wait, and the crowd stamped their feet and slandered him and the sun beat down on their heads to goad them. The chaos nearly came to blows, but Bartholomew refused to fight and would have found himself with a broken nose if the authorities hadn't come and beat the disheveled back with their fists.

The whole ordeal left such a poor taste in his mouth that he sold the whole load of fish to a stall merchant, kept a handful for himself, and then hiked out of the city to get some air. Under the fig tree he unwrapped the oilcloth and took out a wide, flat tilapia and laid it in the grass. He went into the oilcloth again and took out a broad blade knife and staked it through the tail of the fish into the ground. It shone in the sun, cold and dead. He took a paring knife from in his belt and pressed the tip of the blade under the chin of the fish until it snapped through. He drew the blade with some effort down the belly to the tail, cutting out the organs. He spat on the knife and cleaned it against the grass, and he piled the sticky mess to his left. He bent near the fish where it was pinned to the ground and carefully slid the blade against the spine, flaying the skin from the body down to the tail.

From there he took the thick skin in his right hand and peeled it away from the fish, leaving it laid pink and bare and staked to the ground. He pulled the broad blade from the ground and finished skinning both sides, and then carefully laid the fish back into the oilcloth and started on the next.

Within half an hour, the whole basket of fish was cleaned, the fish lined up parallel to one another on the oilcloth with a mound of insides piled to his left that was beginning to attract wasps. The rhythm of it all had calmed him considerably and he let out a sigh. He got up on his knees and dug a shallow hole in the ground and pushed the discards in and covered it with loose soil. He wrapped the bare fish in the cloth and put them back in the basket and leaned against the trunk of the fig tree. For as long as he could remember, the shade of a fig tree had been a place he sought out when he wanted to get away to think and pray. He looked down at the city below him moving like an anthill. The contradiction of the chaos below with the methodic simplicity of preparing his dinner made him contemplative. He wondered at being poor and hungry and at the grief his family and friends had been subjected to in life. He wondered at a world where one man could hate another. The morning had made him feel . . . what? Disappointed, maybe. Hopeful for a better way.

He closed his eyes and tilted his head back against the smooth and twisting bark of the large shady tree. His face felt cool and dry. He thought of the roots below him and how far they must have spread out into the dark earth. How long had it taken for this tree to become what it was? The trunk was easily the breadth of a dozen men, and the roots themselves could have reached for acres as far as he knew. The branches were heavy with fruit and he could smell the sweet figs full and ripe and ready to be gathered. He opened his eyes and scanned the leaves above.

Bartholomew got to his feet and slid off his sandals, and then he reached his arms up overhead and found a low hanging branch and he linked his fingers around it and pulled himself up to his chest. He swung his legs up and over and balanced himself. He reached up with one hand to pull a fig from the leaves near him. It came away with ease and he held it to his nose. The scent was strong and heady and it made him smile. He took a large bite and the juice ran down his chin, and he thought of his boyhood and how he'd spent so many summers hidden in the leaves gorging on good fruit.

He pocketed a few more figs and thought what a good supper he would have that night. He tucked them into the basket beside the fish and gathered up the blades and the basket and made to start down the hill. In the light of the midday sun he saw a figure coming up the hill at a jog. It was Philip, and he was coming toward him at a pace that guaranteed something very good or very bad. Bartholomew imagined Philip had heard that he had sold off his morning's catch. He tucked the basket under his arm and started down the hill to meet Philip where he was and see what had stirred him. —AC

"He wondered at being poor and hungry and at the grief his family and friends had been subjected to in life. He wondered at a world where one man could hate another."

HIS PLACE IN GOD'S STORY

Maintaining that Bartholomew and Nathanael are one and the same, we see a fuller picture of our disciple's place in God's story. When he is told by Philip that the Messiah has come and is from Nazareth, Bartholomew asks how this can be. He understood that, historically, the Messiah would come from Bethlehem. Uniquely, Phillip does not make efforts to explain this away. Instead, he simply tells Bartholomew to come with him and see for himself.

When the two arrive, Jesus, full of grace as usual, makes a point of acknowledging Bartholomew and meeting him in such a way as to affirm him immediately and reassure him that nothing is beyond Him, stating "I saw you while you were still under the fig tree before Philip called you."

As in Jeremiah 29:11, God reminding His people that He did indeed have a hopeful plan for them, so also in John 1:47 Jesus sees our disciple and says to him, "I know you. I know your virtues. And I know what your story has been and will be."

This is the God we serve. A God of order and purpose and patience. We are called to come and experience for ourselves the goodness of God.

THE STORY FINDS ITS PLACE IN ME

1. What parts of Bartholomew's story find their place in you?

2. We live in a global environment that can sometimes seem overwhelmed with the negative. Take a moment to meditate on the times in your life when you've seen God's answers to your prayers.

3. Consider your role in God's promise. How can you be a blessing to others in their daily grind to see God at work?

4. Take a minute to write out your daily routine. Look over the schedule with the intention of seeing it from God's perspective. What do you see in the mundane—the everyday—that you wouldn't notice looking at it from just your perspective? Think, prayerfully about what might be just around the corner for you.

5. In John, Jesus makes it clear to Bartholomew that he knows him, that he is knows his past, present, and future. This is true of all of us. How difficult is it for you to believe this truth on a day-to-day basis? Do your actions display a trust in God's knowledge of the plan?

NOTES